NEW YORK CITY'S FIVE BOROUGHS

NANCY HICER

Rosen Classroom

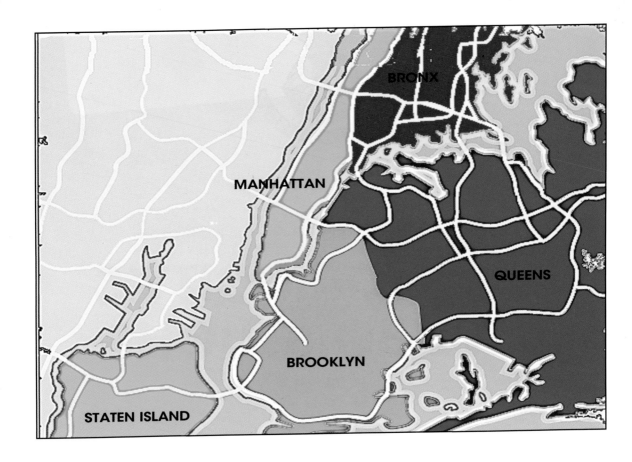

New York City has five **boroughs**. They are Manhattan, Queens, Brooklyn, the Bronx, and Staten Island. Four of these boroughs are on **islands**. Only the Bronx is mostly on the **mainland**.

Manhattan is the oldest of the five boroughs. The name "Manhattan" comes from *Mannahatta*. This means "land of many hills" in the **language** of the Lenape Native Americans who lived on the island long ago.

Manhattan has the most people living in the smallest amount of space. There are 1,634,795 people who live in Manhattan. The Empire State Building is in Manhattan.

Queens is on the western part of Long Island. It was created as a **county** of New York in 1683, when New York was a colony of England. This borough is named for a queen, the wife of King Charles II of England.

Queens has the most amount of land of all five boroughs. It is also home to the second-largest amount of people. Many **immigrants** from all over the world have decided to make Queens their home. Queens is a borough rich in **diversity**.

CITY OF BROOKLYN, L. I.

Taken from Bush Street

In 1630, Dutch **settlers** bought land from the Mohawk Native Americans in what is now a part of Brooklyn. In 1646, the Dutch named this land Breuckelen for a town in the Netherlands, the country they came from.

Brooklyn is home to the most people of all five boroughs. More than 2.5 million people live here. They live in many different **neighborhoods**. In 1883, the Brooklyn Bridge was finished. This helped people go more easily between Brooklyn and Manhattan.

The Bronx River runs through the borough of the Bronx. This river was named for the Swedish settler, Jonas Bronck. In 1639, he bought land between this river and the Harlem River. The borough of the Bronx is named after Bronck's River.

The Bronx is in the northern part of New York City. More than 1,397,287 people live in the Bronx. People from all over the world live in the Bronx. They can go to Yankee Stadium, the Bronx Zoo, Van Cortlandt Park, and Orchard Beach. There are many interesting places in the Bronx.

Staten Island is separated from the other boroughs of New York City by New York **Bay**. More than 491,730 people live on Staten Island. This is the smallest number of people who live in any of the five boroughs. Many people from this borough use the famous Staten Island **Ferry** to go to work in Manhattan.

DEPT. OF TRANSPORTATION   *Staten Island Ferry*   CITY OF NEW YORK

Glossary

bay: a body of water that is mostly surrounded by land

boroughs: the five main parts of New York City

county: an area of a state that is larger than a city and has its own government

diversity: different forms, types, or ideas

ferry: a large boat that goes back and forth between two places

immigrants: people who come to a new country to live

islands: areas of land surrounded by water

language: the speech of a group of people

mainland: a large area of land that does not include islands

neighborhoods: local communities

settlers: people who go to live in a new place where there are few or no people